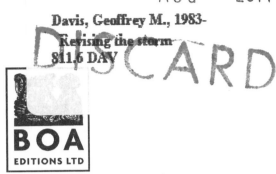

BOA
EDITIONS LTD

REVISING THE STORM

WINNER, 2013 A. POULIN, JR. POETRY PRIZE

SELECTED BY DORIANNE LAUX

Revising the Storm

POEMS BY

GEFFREY DAVIS

FOREWORD BY DORIANNE LAUX

A. Poulin, Jr. New Poets of America Series, No. 36

BOA Editions, Ltd. ⟶ Rochester, NY ⟶ 2014

First Edition
14 15 16 17   7 6 5 4 3 2 1

For information about permission to reuse any material from this book please contact The
Permissions Company at www.permissionscompany.com or e-mail permdude@eclipse.net.

Publications by BOA Editions, Ltd.—a not-for-profit corporation
under section 501 (c) (3) of the United States Internal Revenue
Code—are made possible with funds from a variety of sources,
including public funds from the New York State Council on the
Arts, a state agency; the Literature Program of the National En-
dowment for the Arts; the County of Monroe, NY; the Lannan
Foundation for support of the Lannan Translations Selection Se-
ries; the Mary S. Mulligan Charitable Trust; the Rochester Area
Community Foundation; the Arts & Cultural Council for Greater
Rochester; the Steeple-Jack Fund; the Ames-Amzalak Memorial
Trust in memory of Henry Ames, Semon Amzalak and Dan Amzalak; and contributions
from many individuals nationwide. See Colophon on page 92 for special individual ac-
knowledgments.

ART WORKS.
arts.gov

State of the Arts

NYSCA

Cover Design: Sandy Knight
Cover Art: Malynda Shook
Interior Design and Composition: Richard Foerster
Manufacturing: McNaughton & Gunn
BOA Logo: Mirko

Library of Congress Cataloging-in-Publication Data

Davis, Geffrey M., 1983–
[Poems. Selections]
Revising the storm : poems / by Geffrey Davis ; foreword by Dorianne Laux.
— First Edition.
    pages cm.
ISBN 978-1-938160-28-8 (pbk. : alk. paper)
Includes bibliographical references.
I. Title.
PS3604.A956968A6 2014
811'.6—dc23
                    2013042541

BOA Editions, Ltd.
250 North Goodman Street, Suite 306
Rochester, NY 14607
www.boaeditions.org
A. Poulin, Jr., Founder (1938–1996)

Contents

III. Here a Coursing Wall, There a Slanted House

Foreword

Revising the Storm is one of the best first books I've read in a long time. Its subjects—childhood, an absentee father, marriage, divorce, remarriage, miscarriage, birth—are not new, but the approach is fresh, the language lyrical, the poems well-tuned and masterfully wrought. Geffrey Davis is spellbinding. He knows how to bring even the smallest heartbreaking detail to light. Tenderly but firmly, he leads us down many paths toward the center of a life, as in "What I Mean When I Say *Farmhouse*":

> . . . We have our places for
>
> loneliness—that loaded asking of the body.

The poem concludes:

> I want to jar the tenderness of seasons,
> to crawl deep into the moment. I've come
>
> to write less fear into the boy running
> through the half-dark. I've come for the boy.

Mr. Davis has come for the boy, as well as the man, the distant father. Adept at character study, his people are blushed alive into color and movement. In the course of these tight narratives, he also traverses time and space elegantly, seamlessly:

> In Seattle, in 1982, my mother beholds this man
> boarding the bus, the one she's already
>
> turning into my father. His style (if you can
> call it that): disarming disregard—a loud
>
> Hawaiian-print shirt and knee-high tube socks
> that reach up the deep tone of his legs,
>
> toward the dizzying orange of running shorts.
> Outside, the gray city blocks lurch

past wet windows, as he starts his shy sway
down the aisle. Months will pass

before he shatters his ankle during a Navy drill,
the service discharging him back into the everyday . . .
[from "King County Metro"]

So this is the father, and as much as we will find him wanting, he remains stubbornly human. Coop builder, pigeon lover, testifier, windshield smasher, fisherman, guitar player, truck driver, drug addict, womanizer, newborn cradler, lover of rivers.

Other characters abound in this collection: brothers, mother, cousins, and lovers, all drawn with great precision and skill. One thinks of early Yusef Komunyakaa, one thinks of Li-Young Lee. Carefully chosen, gorgeous images interwoven with statements of pinpoint awareness—one thinks of Mark Doty.

In the end, though, Davis's voice is all his own, with its fraught complexity, its haunted reflecting. Many races mix in these melting-pot poems: African American, Filipino, Irish, and Native American. Family history, struggle and poverty, all are imbued with love and longing, as we watch this young epistemologist encounter "the teeth of the world" and decide on his own definitions.

From "What I Mean When I Say *Truck Driver*":

During the last 50 miles back from haul & some
months past my 15th birthday, my father fishes
a stuffed polar bear from a Salvation Army
gift-bin, labeled *Boys: 6-10*. I can almost see him
approach the decision: cold, a little hungry, not enough

money in his pocket for coffee. He worries
he might fall asleep behind the wheel as his giant,
clumsy love for that small word—*son*—guides
his gaze to the crudely-sewn fabric of the miniature bear
down at the bottom of the barrel. . . .

The poet's quest as a man is to find in his adult life, in his marriage, and in new fatherhood, the seeds of a good life to come. He says to his pregnant wife, as a child might to his own mother:

> . . . *Stay*, I plead, *remain—*

promise not to die. And she does, she vows the impossible multiplication
of her breaths, swears to spend her widowed years splayed like a remainder

caught in the taciturn equation of tomorrow. She gives me her hand 36.5
thousand more times. *Good laps around the sun*, she would say, *still remain*

for us. And we go on like this, forgetting the formulas of our existence.
We make unions from this failure to weigh what may not remain.

And speaking of his wife in "The Discipline of Waking Love":

> kneeling in the garden under the low light of morning,
> waiting for the warmth of her hand upon my back.

Or later, after the birth of their child, from the fine poem "What We Set
in Motion":

> and I send whispers across water, coaching her deeper
> into the swallow of its force, calling it *what we want*,
> calling it *love* or *joy* or *peace*, as in the dark, barely trusting
> each moment that moves her further from this shore,
> where I wait for her, to plant our son into these arms.

It may be, too, that finally the goal of Davis's quest is the man's desire to
heal the past, to "revise the storm," and to look back on the boy and reclaim
him from his lostness and fear and isolation:

> . . . In the dream I realize
> I am your chaperone and button each button
>
> on your dark blue jacket and hold your hand
> a little too tightly, though you make no move
>
> to take it back. How dearly I want to give you
> the gentlest version of my voice, say something
>
> to suspend your belief in disasters . . .
> [from "I Dream of Meeting Myself, Age Seven, County
> Fair Field Trip]

There are delicate, intricate poems here, stormed by memory, always in motion. If the family is the greatest catastrophe, it is also the source of our most profound joy. Geffrey Davis reminds us how to survive and endure both.

—Dorianne Laux

for my siblings and my son, especially . . .

We suffer each other to have each other a while.

—Li-Young Lee

In the parable,
like the dream, you're all the characters,
though come the day, in real life, you must choose.

—Stanley Plumly

I.

THE BOOK OF FATHER

What I Mean When I Say *Farmhouse*

Time's going has ebbed the moorings
to the memories that make this city-kid

part farm-boy. Until a smell close enough to
the sweet-musk of horse tunes my ears back

to tree frogs blossoming after a country rain.
I'm back among snakes like slugs wedged

in ankle-high grass, back inside that small
eternity spent searching for soft ground, straining

not to spill the water-logged heft of a drowned
barn cat carried in the shallow scoop of a shovel.

And my brother, large on the stairs, crying.
Each shift in the winds of remembering renders me

immediate again, like ancient valleys reignited
by more lightning. If only I could settle on

the porch of waiting and listening,
near the big maple bent by children and heat,

just before the sweeping threat of summer
thunderstorms. We have our places for

loneliness—that loaded asking of the body.
My mother stands beside the kitchen window, her hands

no longer in constant motion. And my father
walks along the tired fence, watching horses

and clouds roll down against the dying light—
I know he wants to become one or the other.

I want to jar the tenderness of seasons,
to crawl deep into the moment. I've come

to write less fear into the boy running
through the half-dark. I've come for the boy.

King County Metro

In Seattle, in 1982, my mother beholds this man
boarding the bus, the one she's already

turning into my father. His style (if you can
call it that): disarming disregard—a loud

Hawaiian-print shirt and knee-high tube socks
that reach up the deep tone of his legs,

toward the dizzying orange of running shorts.
Outside, the gray city blocks lurch

past wet windows, as he starts his shy sway
down the aisle. Months will pass

before he shatters his ankle during a Navy drill,
the service discharging him back into the everyday

teeth of the world. Two of four kids will arrive
before he meets the friend who teaches him

the art of roofing and, soon after, the crack pipe—
the attention it takes to manage either

without destroying the hands. The air brakes gasp
as he approaches my mother's row,

each failed rehab and jail sentence still
decades off in the distance. So much waits

in the fabulous folds of tomorrow.
And my mother, who will take twenty years

to burn out her love for him, hesitates a moment
before making room beside her—the striking

brown face, poised above her head, smiling.
My mother will blame all that happens,

both good and bad, on this smile, which glows now,
ready to consume half of everything it gives.

Revising the Storm, 1991

—for E

I.

This childhood memory sneaks up on me, little Brother,
like the storm that summer afternoon. I could be thinking

of a color, a girl, and suddenly it will be there, large
and gray and waiting for accuracy. Most details I get right: how,

days earlier, the baler—perhaps in a rush, perhaps distracted
by anticipations of evening flesh—left the bales of hay too close

for the flatbed to pass between. And so the men told us to roll hay
to be muscled away from the storm, from the coming rain that

threatened every mouth on the farm—my arms eight years old, yours seven,
neither strong enough to stay ahead of the truck. But this is where my . . .

I was going to say *memory fails me*, but perhaps I mean something more
immediate, more violent, like *pride* or *shame* that cuts through

this remembering. Was it I who lost nerve and fled as the first
raindrops fell and lightning downed the large maple just beyond the pasture?

Or did your eyes apologize as you turned weeping for the house?
In our retelling, I always stay, though we've left out the part where

I cry after you're gone, certain that catching me alone like that,
brotherless and soaked with rain, felt like vengeance—easy, human.

II.

We have grown so thin, Brother. And, today, that thinness makes
these going clouds seem desperate in their going.

I know to blame the wind and not the clouds, which might be a metaphor
for our love, because I cannot help but feel a similar hurt wonderment—

that they go so far, that they grow so thin.

III.

What would it mean to revise this memory? Perhaps we could return to some
first faith, some uninterrupted union. Let us turn memory's blade

against ourselves, harness that constant crisis to improve the current
          state of things
between us. Let me forever be the one who watches you weep from beneath
the eaves of the farmhouse, whose young guts split with the thundered air.

I want to be forgiven now. I need you to know that I have already returned
to your side, embarrassed and ready again to face down the storm.

Instructions for a Fourth-Grade Report on Texas

Grab the card stock from teacher's desk,
as quickly as you can.

Grab the necessary crayons. Get in line and hope hard that
nobody claims your father's state before
you reach the front.

Smile when you see the empty column beside *Texas*.
When the teacher hands you its history and symbols,
relax. Slip them into your backpack—keep them perfect.

Rush home to memorize the details before your father returns:
the bustle of Austin, the treacherous Rio Grande,
Pecan Trees (*Carya illinoinensis*) weighted with false nuts,
and regal plumes of Bluebonnet (*Lupinus subcarnosus*) flooding
the meadows where Mockingbirds (*Mimus polyglottos*) pick through
the sounds of spring.

Color each broad square of the flag's design
and the solo star—use the white crayon, finally.

Color the seal's five celestial points the universal yellow
you have learned, and the olive and oak branches
a flattened green beneath the sprawling "State of Texas."

Trace as best you can, by eye, a silhouette of its borders,
of land floating in space. Fill in terrain.
Think about your father as a boy, between low
mountain ranges and rugged hills. Think of rattlesnakes.

Wait for your father at the kitchen table. Watch
as he touches a callused finger to his childhood
between the boundaries you've drawn.

Call the project done. Go to school proud.

Hold back hurt in your stomach when
Alicia from the front row points at your map,
says, *It looks like a heart—a real one.*

Meaning, all your effort looks like the wrong
and right thing.

Meaning, your image for father has become this fistlike
force that keeps your insides in motion.

What I Mean When I Say *Chinook Salmon*

My father held the unspoken version of this story
along the bridge of his shoulders: *This is how*
we face and cast to the river—at angles.
This is how we court uncertainty. Here, he taught
patience before violence—to hold, and then
to strike. My fingers carry the stiff

memory of knots we tied to keep a 40-lb. King
from panicking into the deep current
of the stream. Back home, kneeling
at the edge of the tub with our kills, he showed
the way to fillet a King: slice into the soft
alabaster of the pectoral, study the pink-rose notes

from the Pacific, parse waste and bone from flesh. Then,
half asleep, he'd put us to bed, sometimes with kisses.

The Epistemology of Birds

My niece stood one morning
at the border of knowing *sparrow*

as a compact crash into the living-room
window, and in the wake of that noise

I turned ten again, pointing my BB-gun
at birds, ignorant of the seconds

up ahead—the sudden swerve
of consequence. I no longer recall

which species, just their tawny toes
nearly invisible against the branch.

Taking aim, I coveted their movements,
their defiance of space and time,

as when what I can't forget: the first one
I hit from a limb, its fall a burnt struggle—

half against sky, half against ground,
and me half expecting to see it

denounce both and gravity and cut
across the world again, like visible wind.

Instead, it finished, fell, and then I had
feathers against the green grass

and my embarrassed desire to have it
fly back inside the tree. And so,

when that sparrow struck the shadow
of my niece's curiosity, I did what I could

to mute that blunt arrival:—rushed outside,
gently scooped the broken-necked

and headed toward the alley, to hide it
beneath a week's worth of garbage

and newspapers, searching on my return
for a different image of *bird*.

What I Mean When I Say *My Name Is Nobody*

In a room tucked inside a neighborhood of fist-fights and hard drugs, my father rewinds scenes from his favorite Spaghetti Western, in which legends arise from the silly stuff. He points out the facial expressions and antics of the mock-hero: young Nobody, untouchable in his clownish triumphs and self-parody. My father hunches with laughter when Nobody disarms the hardened intentions of the murderous Wild Bunch gang with his blond-haired, blue-eyed absurdity. Meanwhile, the aging hero-hero, Jack Beauregard, the callous lawman whose name everyone knows, has tasted the bitter grit of good-versus-evil. He's grown tired of hard-winning the odds stacked against him. He wants a warm shave without the insurance of a pistol pointed at the groin of the barber, to not find the family tied up in the soap closet, that the barber's a fake again, another anonymous assassin from the Wild Bunch that he must outsmart and gun down. We understand this means no smiling for Jack, only his deferred pleasure in feeling the skin along his neck tingle at the tenderness of a friendly bladed hand. And it goes on and on like this—our heroes must continually outdraw themselves. The ambushes get serious: the gunslingers begin aiming for the back and waiting for Jack to fall sleep, and now he needs another gun and a set of eyes behind him to make it out alive. Eventually, Jack tries shrugging off the latest murders. He submits to the slow decline in his vision and boards a boat back to anonymity, leaving behind his big white cowboy hat for Nobody. All the while, my father rewinds and rewinds, his laughter leavening and leaving our house.

Call Me Now

—to my cousin

Take us then: two black boys plus the poverty line.
Take the 90s—we carried scratched rap
CDs concealed in bomber jackets,
sagged in baggy jeans and cocked
our hats backwards, in some small defiance
of the waking knowledge that a future
was barreling our way, possibility's obscurity
fast behind it. Add the fathers we feared
becoming: stern fathers, who forgot to hug;
weak fathers, who forgot to hug. Add mothers
pinned beneath the never-ending work-week.

Then raise it all to the power of 3:00 a.m.
commercials with psychics giving better shapes
to tomorrow, for the full price of eggs, a gallon of milk
per minute. I still envy that you caved first
to the weight of your curiosity at the numinous bodies
we might burst into, that your voice, even then,
had a well deep enough to sound *18-or-older*. "Fuck it,"
you mumbled and picked up the phone, clearing
the music in your throat. I tuned in
on a muted cordless, as you accepted
the charges for balancing the problem.

Factor in the operator who caught
the boy in your voice. Subtract her clairvoyant gaze,
but keep the costs: *Call back when you're older,*
hon'. How could we calculate knowing
what we feared would be set into a fleshy stone,
would be canceled out with other worries?
Although our mothers wore us out when
the phone bill arrived, I still carry the messy
formulas from those nights of testing touch-tone

combinations to the future: 1-800-
PLEASE   1-800-WHO-CAN-WE-BE?

Unfledged

What did I know, what did I know
of love's austere and lonely offices?
                    —Robert Hayden

Weekends too my father roofed poor neighborhoods,
at prices only his back could carry

into profit. In the name of labor's
virtue—or was it another bill collector's callous

calling again?—my brother and I became
his two-boy cleanup crew. During those hard,

gloved hours under the sun's weight, I studied
my father, from the ground—the distance he kept

between us his version of worry. This work gave him
chance to patch over his latest night in county jail, to shout

over something other than his drug-heavy belly song.
More than witnessing the way he knew a hammer,

more than the sweat, the grace of his body grew
when I noticed the cheap pigeon magazines tucked

in his back pocket—black & white photos
of pedigreed squabs he'd fallen for, folded

for a later that never came: the careful study we do
with things that refuse to become ours.

Evenings, he tended to his own homemade
kit-box of birds, bathed in the constant coos

from a mongrel mix of orphaned Birmingham rollers
and hand-captured homers that he bred the distance out of,

turning our block into the new destination
their blood pulled them toward. On the job,

from below, as he perched and drove nails through
the day's heat, I checked the silhouetted length of his back

for signs of stiffness, and his impossible arms, anything
I might point to—certain, like most people,

if the ache could be found, you'd know
how to start soothing, where to place your hands.

What I Mean When I Say *Roller Pigeon*

The reason behind this breed's midair acrobatics
        splits its admirers: *evasion evolution* or *neural defect?*

. . . though they agree on the sanctity
        of that tight, feathered backspin.

Whatever the catalyst—feint against
        the ghostly hawk, against the sudden spec-

tacular falcon, or the brain's spotty electric
        refusal to soar—I could imagine an addiction

to that falling away. Enter ERROR of desire.
        Enter FATHER with the wild roller pigeons

he caught beneath highway overpasses. I held
        a flashlight as he bagged them at night,

as he spread the sheen of their wings under the glow,
        in love with the way they gave themselves

over to that plummet—and then, just as easy,
        their return to the flock's steady orbit.

I stayed close to my father's hip when
        fanciers warned him of breeding

for the fall, of mating his deepest rollers together
        so he could witness those long twists

down to earth—how our obsessions can turn
        the miracle against itself.

That first, fated dive to make impact with a rooftop
        sounded so much smaller than I expected—

and the silence that followed, barely there: two or three
      beats before my father began his panicked

come home-clap, urging that crumpled star to struggle
      back into the open arms of the air.

What I Mean When I Say *Elijah-Man*

> *And it came to pass, [...] there appeared a chariot of fire*
> *and horses of fire, and parted them both asunder; and Elijah*
> *went up by a whirlwind into heaven. And Elisha saw it,*
> *and he cried, My father, my father . . .*
>   —2 Kings 2:11–12

That Sunday in Chehalis, my father testified
and I watched as he wept before the pulpit,

his shoulders heaving, his hands
clapping up thunder above our heads,

his mouth open on the note of awe as he told us
the promise God had made in the dream:

to bring him Home before he tasted death . . .
to wake him with the scent of flowers, proof

of His presence. I learned to cry like that, as if
I could sprain the heart, the body hurting its way out.

But that morning my mind snuck
back to the nights he took paychecks and split,

sometimes for weeks, his head and body
humming for dope, his wife and kids

suspended by the boundlessness of waiting.
If he returned, if his pockets were empty,

if the locks had been changed, I'd watch
from the window as he jumped and hollered,

wide-eyed and ripping the gate from its hinges or
shattering the windshields of cars along our street

with his fists—how, as the sirens drew near,
not even God could stop him.

A Poem for God

I still weigh the nights I spent
shattered by headaches, pitched inside

my mother's sleepless arms, the undiagnosed
splashes on brain scans, and my father's whispers

working my temples like regret. I remember
the warm burden of Your congregation's hands

laid on me in prayer, and the calm confusion
that spread on doctors' faces when my follow-ups

turned clear. I walked from the hospital
a miracle-boy. By Sunday morning,

my father swore he had the end of his affliction
in sight, as he carried me into Your House

and presented me to the flock—: But You know
I lied, ignored the pain folding my thoughts,

lasted the long nights alone, twisted in my bed.
Still I stood inside Your pulpit, poised: the wound-free

proof—my tender head offered up as if the fleshy
fruit of faith. (Decades later, from time to time,

that old pounding slips back between my ears
like an intimacy.) And so I have few words

for You that share the same ragged tones
my father used to beg away his broken spirit,

filling the rooms of our house with God,
his dog-eared bible between his knees, all night,

the tears falling. And outside You look like the sun
turning the green of the West, the green that

I love, the color of ache. The given
and the taken away—God: the question

in my father's voice, graveled with grief,
under the slow-sick spread of Your morning's light.

More Than Forgery

I.

In middle school, I practiced
signing my father's name, for days,

filled empty sheets of paper secretly in class,
comparing his graceful autograph to the frauds.

The beginning tripped me up—the capital A—
his detail so hard to copy: the tight flourish

of ink just before the first downstroke of the pen.
Because I worried over penmanship, because,

like him, I favored an unfinished cursive,
I watched my forgeries lean toward the real thing

before endorsing the backs of his V. A. checks,
piled up during the months he vanished into rehabs

or chased fixes: *Pay to the order of* food to hush
our rumblings. The checks kept us

in lights and warm water.

II.

                    Or the way my father
tapped his foot while playing the guitar: he kept

a different, distant beat—the one to play against.
The lyrics he belted became wounds riding the air

and left me, the boy who wished and wept for birds,
fighting off tears so he would sing another hour.

By high school, I knew he'd left for good.
His *A* stayed in my hand.

It flares up in every *Adam* or *Alinique*
I write—in every love letter I end, *Always yours.*

What I Mean When I Say *Truck Driver*

During the last 50 miles back from haul & some
months past my 15th birthday, my father fishes
a stuffed polar bear from a Salvation Army
gift-bin, labeled *Boys: 6-10*. I can almost see him
approach the decision: cold, a little hungry, not enough

money in his pocket for coffee. He worries
he might fall asleep behind the wheel as his giant,
clumsy love for that small word—*son*—guides
his gaze to the crudely-sewn fabric of the miniature bear
down at the bottom of the barrel. Seasons have flared

& gone out with little change in his fear of stopping
for too long in any city, where he knows the addict
in him waits, patient as a desert bloom. Meanwhile, me:
his eldest child, the uneasy guardian of the house.
In his absence, I've not yet lost my virginity,

but I've had fist-fights with grown men & seen
my mother dragging her religious beliefs to the bitter
border of divorce. For years my father's had trouble
saying *no* to crack-cocaine & women flowered in cheap
summer dresses. Watch his face as he arrives at last

& stretches the toy out, my mother fixed
on the porch behind me, the word *son* suddenly heavy
in my father's mouth, his gray coat gathered
around his shoulders: he's never looked so small.
We could crush him—we hug him instead.

What My Father Might Say, If I Let Him Speak

Son: I stayed spooning your mother's
softly snoring form, as she swelled with you,
month after month. Your voice pierced

the Seattle spring air, and I began to wake
in the early hours, before work, my mind
and body dragged from that otherworldly

cavern of sleep, to watch you flexing your life.
I biked three miles home on lunch breaks
to bottle feed you, begged your mother

to make you wait. Stop turning these details
toward a genesis for a lifetime of hanging on.
I showed you what the living can do

and call love—that a man can rise, coughing
from the ashes of himself,
and go back down again, like prayer.

My Last Love Poem for a Crackhead, #23

Some nights I hear my father's long romance
with drugs echoed in the skeletal choir

of crickets. At each approach, a silence
cuts in. And I wonder which part speaks more

to this dance with addiction: the frailty of concord
or the hard certainty of the coda's chain?

I know these are only insects being insects,
merely a strumming of lust into the heavy,

summer air. Still, something in me asks for
a new piece of music to yoke to his cravings—

perhaps just the need to shuffle off and sing
my own restlessness back to sleep.

I want him to be beautiful again.
He fucked us over—he did, but breakdown

diminishes everyone. Let me decide
that he never lied or stole more than necessary.

From the Unsent Letters: To Klamath Falls Correctional Facility

—for my father

Because I rescued this bird the other day
      from the lethal humidity of a parking deck stairwell

Because it didn't take much effort:
      fifteen minutes spent in the easy
      feel-good of not continuing on my way

Because I admit here, after releasing the bird back into the toothy elements,
      back against the sharp shadows of the day,
      I didn't stay for long

Because I didn't even check the woodwind of its battered wings
      for fractures—

Because I never witnessed the bird catch
      the breath it had lost while knocking the acoustics
      of its skull against concrete

Because I still want the undeserved ease of mind

Because I need for you and the bird to survive, despite the odds,
      and for this noise to sing us on our way, toward anything
      but the silences that we know

Because I think of you, of how you could stand for hours,
      looking up into that air,
      and no bird pass by

II.

DIASPORA

The Newakum River

I have been here before, smelled the same greenness and named it
fishing, my other religion. I've seen the river bent and falling,
trees bowed along the muddy banks, an early fog hovering

above the water's current, like some gray ghost out over
the going body. Here each cast is *prayer*, each slacked retrieval
prayer denied. I have prayed this way since my father taught me,

since he showed me *prayer answered* in the brilliant scales of trout,
salmon, steelhead. And now I return, trying to recreate
the warm miracle—to pull the bulletlike answers from below.

Write the Memory of Throwing the Stone

—for C

Tell it right this time. Don't wonder whether
    you took aim,

        whether, at eight, you could choose
to send that wound through the air,

          with a perfect arch,
    into the skull of your baby brother.

    In fact, tell this:
nothing provoked it—he never saw it

    coming. Remember how you emptied
your hands and rushed to his animal noise,

            dropping down to be with him,
    pinned by pain and wailing,

the frozen winter grass stinging your knees.
    You wept the long vowels of grief,

both your broken sounds striking a new
        center of the universe—

          its gravity pulled
back histories and ideas like sheets,

    leaving you all nerves
        and naked feelings.

Remember lifting his small weight from the ground
        and the shock of the moment's passing:

the danger of you taking your places again,
back among the living—the hurt you created, as children do,

by accident and on purpose,
already fading from your brother's eyes.

Teaching Twelve-Year-Olds the Trail of Tears

Take a book and pass them back. Turn to
the pencil-line sketches of soldiers, more
gunpoint than reason, a darkness aimed

at a different darkness. *It was an odd kind of murder—
the killing of hope*, blanketed backs and wagons
diminishing into a ribbon of exiled dots

among the thickening smoke of 1838. Matt, stop
drawing on school property. Memorize the map, Class,
all eight inches of hashed texture—one for every

hundred miles of terrain, pocked by makeshift graves—
and the legend, with its color-coded routes: dark-blue
broken lines of sorrow hurried along water. Tanya,

this note says your father waits for you in the office.
Bye-bye. Before recess, write down statistics for mothers
marching on under the weight of dead newborns

in their arms. Fill in bar graphs for the elderly
slumped beside the way—this, the morbid geometry
of their torsos, folded by dysentery.

Repeat after me: *They arrived almost without children
and with few elders, with almost no past and no future.*
Now, have a good lunch. Behave. Michael, no running.

Venison

In my previous life as a deer, I honed my brand
of nervousness, balanced instinct and memory,

sharpened that ability to slip silently between
thicket and meadow, changing from fluid motion

to some frozen effigy of the thing—: existence
reduced to traveling my predispositions. Poised

over the hard hoof, I tested the live weight of
never feeling all the way prepared, searched out

spoiled apples beneath winter's ice, at a moment
ready to morph into a fleeing patch of white

haunch among the naked trees. I raced against
the hunter's success, against the day

he would hit the muskiness of my hide
and the hot, mercurial life beneath it—: carve me,

freeze me, the velvet vastness of my body
parceled out to loved ones, in easily stored pieces.

How Can I Be 1/32nd Blackfeet?

—for J. Brunoe

"Bloodline too-little-known," "band scattered like leaves":—
Unable to find my father, I lost my place
on the Dawes Rolls, failed my quantum,
had my federal CDIB card revoked.
In CA, I bloomed beneath the tropical bends
in my mother's family tree, twisted with emigration.

In WA, where the Douglas firs sway
in the deep shadows of the Rockies,
I dreamt of taproots held in the lean grip
of ancestral grasslands. By the time I wandered
into OR, into the warm wood of the Long House,
the word "Indian" sat dried and muted on my tongue.

Who was it that called this tendency to fall apart *Native*,
this inclination for doubt *beautiful*?

If the Moon Were My Lover

It would be difficult to depend
on her pallid skin—her drifting, sickly light—
to avoid envy when finding her
held in the grassy arms of meadows,
long-pressed against bodies of water,
or running through human hair

not mine. In school, our teachers gave her to us
in phases, taught us her tendency to wax
and wane into far-off gibbous arches,
her absence an illusion of the deeper darks.
Perhaps I could learn to ignore my moon softly
rolled in the mouths of men and women.

Perhaps I would return each night at tide-turn,
only dare her to do the things I know she will do.

What I Mean When I Say *Diaspora*

*Longing, we say, because desire is full
of endless distances.*

—Robert Hass

If I pull time back to 1997, I can see my father tiptoeing
on the edge of chances. He's afraid again of the hard drugs

and a new thinness to his body. This year he gets himself
licensed for long-haul and leaves behind the deep green

of our Puget Sound, placing another last bet on sobriety.
As sixteen big-rig tires put Idaho between him and every

dope dealer he's ever known, Montana seems to show herself,
and so he leaves the FM radio off, taking solitude with him

through two more states. Months go by before he's down
in Pecos, stirring up his own father in the Texas dust.

His childhood house looks the same from outside:
single-storied, sun-paled, and fenced. When the screen door

cracks, the familiar smack of booze fills my father's head,
and he smiles his boyish smile, waiting for the slow wave

of recognition to arrive on the face buoyed before him. But
his own father—alone and drunk, a little shrunken now

and showing the gray sag of time in his shoulders—does
not recognize him, cannot see the same high cheekbones.

Swaying there in the hard-corner arms of the doorway,
his father sees him as *stranger*, come for food or money,

and curses him off the front porch when he says something
sentimental like, *You, Daddy—I think I need you.*

My father sits inside his cab and cries. And then
he knocks again, this time with creased photos in hand.

And that is it—: my grandfather opens the door
a little wider, and my father looks along the faded walls—

the rows of pictures my mother has been sending
from Washington all these years: our fixed, smiling faces.

My Mother's Uncle

How seamlessly we try to slip back into the fallowing lives
of the distant, dying relatives—more precious in their dying.

My mother, who bows near his deathbed, has not seen Cary
since the 80s. All morning she's suffered the elder cousins

flaunting the coconut tones of their Filipino skin, cutting her
out with broken bits of a language she's never learned.

When she understands that Cary will not recognize her face again,
that the morphine has left him all body, all groans and waves

of cancered pain, she slips from the hospital room. On the phone,
I listen again to her handful of memories, hear her consoled

by the faithful rise and fall of her own voice, the narrative currents
as familiar as a childhood river—so charted by her retellings.

In each story, she's a little girl: the one where Cary surprise
visits, but her mother has gone out for groceries and so

she must say, sadly, from the window, that she cannot answer
the door. Cary, of course, smiles before turning to go, passes up

three pieces of her favorite rice candy, and tells her she is
good girl. In another story, she runs into his workshop

in tears, because the cousins will not stop teasing, will not
stop chanting *pangit balat*, of which she understands only the dark

shadow of intention, and it works. All those decades ago,
Cary did not dry her freckled face before shepherding her

back into the living room for apologies—her lightly tanned hand
led toward reunion by the deep texture and warmth of his own.

The Epistemology of Hospitals

I have yet to survey the Irish grit
of my grandmother's hands, to ask after her first
stumbles with needle and thread—the awkward outline

of butterflies drifting the pillowcase. I've struggled
to conjure the deftness of her youthful fingers
thrust between the thorns, as she ate blackberries

straight from the bramble. I've wished I memorized
more—her tenor of silence, say—or chanced being
the grandchild crouched at the crack in the kitchen door,

catching her voice in song while fudge baked
in the winter. I search for her bones in the morning
mirror, her eyes wet with memory. I invent the stories

she's meant to tell: miniskirts, record high temps,
and swimming nude all one summer—dive after
graceful dive from the boulders lining the river.

The Epistemology of Gentleness

—for R

When you're in love with someone
whose father has committed suicide, you demand

that the world be gentle with her now.
The world, of course, will not listen.

Still you go through the motions—smile to her,
assure her of the small, human ways the world

will bend softly, now that you have set it straight.
And suddenly, to spite you, suicide shows up

everywhere. No story is safe, and people
these days will kill themselves over anything:

the home-team loss, stalled traffic, sappy love songs
overplayed on the radio. You find yourself turning

the conversations, the channels, storming out together
midway through movies. At the rental store, hand in hand,

you learn to predict nooses and medicine cabinets,
suicidal tendencies coded in DVD descriptions.

And you lie: *The reviews got this one all wrong*—or
—I've seen this one, darling. It would put us both to sleep.

The Epistemology of Marriage

They hurry down the hallway's ruin,
avoiding the rooms that they can—the domestic
wreckage, the storm's everywhere dark not quite
dispersed. Tomorrow they will spackle
the hole beside the stairs and pick
what glass they can from the carpet, the couch,

the basket of clean laundry. For now,
exhausted or embarrassed, the thunder lowered
to a mumble in the far corners of this valley,
they hesitate beside the bed. Before turning back
the comforter and crawling together
beneath the sheets, they clear the blades

from their hands—the better to clench each other
and what light lingers in the day.

Divorce Means

Her body surrendering tension in twitches—
sudden spring, lightning rain, and the rabbit
we crushed along the highway. At night,

sometimes, I find her in handfuls and
mouthfuls of brown hair. But under this
half-light, although she's fought it, she rocks shut

to the rhythm of her father's slow sway
from a garage rafter. And I can't lead us back
to the old silences. I refuse to be the spilled wine

on the grass. Like her, I've never left Tacoma:
I am still the young boy praying inside
an abandoned white pickup, the cab strangely

hallowed beneath a yellow street lamp—and I want
to curl up beside my missing father,
stoned on a crackhouse couch. Our moments

remain infinite for having happened.
We became the covered bridge in the morning,
and the wandering stream beneath it. But

one of us tilted slightly, turning more
wooden bridge in the blame of the day's
brutal light, the other more watery stream.

From 35,000 Feet / Praise Aviophobia

The vivid sunset, the sky's venous blue
        as it rages to orange, to arterial red—

I read faith there, some shared exploit of blood.
        What of the mercurial circuitry

of the cityscape below? At night, from 35,000 feet
        of sight, the viral light we cast seems

held against extinction. So who cares about
        a little nervous circling of the runway

or the way some turbulence will pull at the body
        from within and betray the smallness

of these hands gripping the armrest? I will bear
        the heavenly soupiness of the clouds,

forgive the pilot's jagged descent into it.
        Praise aviophobia and my brutal desire

for contact, for skin again and every lover
        I have caressed. This be the blessèd

in-between, the holy fall from the flock,
        from the union-whole . . .

until the touch to ground, when I resist my urge
        to hug and kiss the stranger there beside me.

Meditation at a Pennsylvania Diner: Early Morning

—for R

I order cranberry juice with my over-easy eggs
and wheat toast: an impulse that lingers

from my ex-wife's concern for my body
and what it could not hold forever.

What does it mean to name this moment
concord? With thousands of miles, three

ranges of mountains, and a merciless silence
between us, let this drink-order simply bless

this morning headed West, her way, still fat
with possibility. My waiter's smile seems

convincing enough. He's kept my coffee warm
and the toast arrives unburnt. Yes, just kids,

we failed utterly to span that great domestic divide—
we didn't have a chance—but I applaud those two

for staying in it until the house burned
to the ground. And now, if only for her

ghostly part in ensuring I have enough
cranberry juice to wash it all down, I wish her

100% of her daily vitamins when she wakes,
a healthy portion of phytochemical nutrients

and antioxidants—glasses of juice so fresh
she could sing of a deliciousness to this world.

I refuse the false concentrate this diner uses
to become some dark hearkening to our misplaced

faith in the deep red promise of wetland blossoms.
We have every spring to recover,

to gulp the aroma of blooms—lungs filled with
the spectral sweetness of fruit we will never eat.

Write the Memory of the Girl Dancing in Apple Blossoms

—for N

Tell how, in the orchard's middle, the petals just rained
          down as she danced around the trunk of the tree.

                              Describe her arms,
raised into the Y of worship or request.

                    Although you knew better,
it looked as if she held up the sky,

                              as if she'd conjured the tree
and its sudden shedding of pink-white blossoms. Then

          you noticed the father
                              in the branches above, smiling.

Remember how uncertain you became—if he knew
          the miracle he was making,
          if he could feel her arms suspend him there.

6th Avenue Flora

—for my mother

That flower-crazed summer, when even the wind
would not let up, we children thought we had

affection figured. Scouring alleys
and parkways, we stuffed jelly containers

and baby-food jars with fists of buttercups,
dandelion heads, purple-pale calyxes

of clover. Caught up in our urgency
to express, we went blocks without permission,

traveled south to gather the noxious wild carrot
and Scotch broom, brought back thistle blossoms—

our worship quickly becoming a kind of injury
waiting to happen. Before long, someone returned

with flowers too large or too vibrant to be
city weeds, snatched in rapture from pristine

gardens of north-side strangers. And so we,
like everyone, learned that love may occasion

damage—How determined to offer any petal
poised above the pavement. How sweetly bound.

III.

HERE A COURSING WALL,
THERE A SLANTED HOUSE

I Dream of Meeting Myself, Age Seven, County Fair Field Trip

From far off at first: you, alone
on the playground or walking intently

toward the buses loading for the spring fair,
your brow furrowed—already a serious face

with no adults around. In the dream I realize
I am your chaperone and button each button

on your dark blue jacket and hold your hand
a little too tightly, though you make no move

to take it back. How dearly I want to give you
the gentlest version of my voice, say something

to suspend your belief in disasters:
you, in your old man's sweater and analog

wristwatch. I know you are not eating well,
that you hear our mother crying in the kitchen

some nights, and spend such nights training yourself
to steady the tooth of hunger—to tame

that animal tug of the guts. Admit your hunger.
Let me steer you toward concession stands,

pick one of everything off the menu: caramel apples,
the mysterious elephant ear, all six shades

of cotton candy, an onion burnt
to bloom. Before I make my mouth

say any of this, before I open my arms
for the unsolicited hug, you throw me

that little-man smile of yours: you, releasing my hand,
already on your way toward becoming me.

The Epistemology of Rosemary

—for L

Together in the garden, a cigarette cradled
between her fingers, she tells me of breeding

cockatiels—clutch after successful clutch, and what
she can't forget: the time of one-too-many and

the smallest chick pushed from the nest.
How she thought *mistake* and put it back again,

only to see the same, simple denial.
And then, for days, trying to make her hands

avian, to syringe-feed the bird into flight.
One thin month lies between us and our miscarriage,

and I feel her grow silent under the new vastness
of this wreckage. I try to talk about my father

breaking blighted pigeon eggs: at twelve, I thought
patience and pressed him to wait, one week, then two,

until frustration set and he crushed the shells
before me, against the coop. I wanted to gather up

each shard, to will those gossamer embryos
into growth again—   What do we rescue

now, at home, gleaning herbs in the evening,
as swallows swerve in the fallow air? I lean over

her shoulder: her hair smells of the rosemary we take,
and of the rosemary we leave to freeze in the garden.

Farmer's Market Sweet Plums: Apology to the Flower Lady

We have no issue with her, *per se*. Guilty,
we knew already what we wanted
long before we noticed the slow gesture
of her fingers: flower to scissors, to vase,
to flower again. Her painful carefulness—:
that anonymous labor for more

beauty *qua* beauty. She almost convinces us
to forget the fruit and choose the flower
in her hands:—to take from her
that burden of belief. Leaving the market,
with bags of plums bumping at our hips, we begin
to offer strangers that rounded sweetness,

one by one, desperate for her gentleness,
for her certainty in what the living need.

Dear Destruction

Months after our miscarriage, you still
recoil from my caress, and I keep

noticing your lift from bed—no
graceful wobble toward the bathroom,

no world inside to set you slightly off

balance. And if I tell you that I weep
quietly into our sheets? I want to steal the stone

in your voice, to silence the ultrasound
technician before she can reframe

our baby as "blighted ovum."

Enter CLUMSY SAVAGERY.
Enter DEAR DESTRUCTION and the malignant

aftermath we've inherited, surrendering
the promises that we practiced

marveling and waking to: back *motherhood*,
back *fatherhood*, back the morning's song.

Like This, For a Reason

How to find the tender underbelly
of grief, to turn it down

onto its side, so you can hold it,
kiss it and rename it:

my mother taught this. The lost dog
became *patience*. And finding it

dead along the road meant *go ahead and cry now.*
But then, with her fingers spread

against our sobbing chests, *we feel pain
large like this for a reason.*

Each month, the money thinned
and she stood alone in the kitchen

humming the last bit of our food
into *songs of tomorrow . . .*

Even her cataracted eye, the one
my father punched years ago,

setting the unhurried cloud into motion,
we've since claimed as victory.

Though, before the surgery,
she never mentioned an absence of color—

the hues fading slowly enough
to manage the heart's break. *Everything's so soft,*

she'd say, and meant it: the sharp dive of green
growing shallower in the Sound,

cornflower blue calming itself
shade by shade,

the keys of yellow muted to a familiar
flatness she called *spring*.

Ode to Trout

O my coy darlings, still you wear for me
the possibilities of this world's

wasted pallet. Down in the valley,
your broken-up browns bend

toward this born-again orange.
And you speckle the ice-

cold spring waters woven
between the thinning high pine forests.

Look here!—
who but you could survive your long-ago,

lacerated throat, its urgent red now
buried in your jaw and painted at your cheeks?

When I hold you in these coastal hands,
I risk keeping you from carrying the rainbow

that life has shot you through with
back into the vast Pacific—

from casting your small spark
against the terrible depths.

What I Mean When I Say *Forever*

This messy mathematics of memory, this overlooking of remainders—
we divide our loved ones from the interplay of seasons. What remainders

we recount we'll spread like petals at their feet. Later, I may even add
a little bit of wind to the ordinariness of this day, if only so she'll remain

as taut with life as she is now, dancing on the lawn between cigarettes,
the threat of subtraction pressed between her lips. *Stay*, I plead, *remain*—

promise not to die. And she does, she vows the impossible multiplication
of her breaths, swears to spend her widowed years splayed like a remainder

caught in the taciturn equation of tomorrow. She gives me her hand 36.5
thousand more times. *Good laps around the sun*, she would say, *still remain*

for us. And we go on like this, forgetting the formulas of our existence.
We make unions from this failure to weigh what may not remain.

The Discipline of Waking Love

—for L

Because I wake early and easy: at the jangle of dog collar
in the next room or a thought landing louder than sleep—

and because she does not; she wakes in parts, over and over again—
I have learned patience when trying to rouse her.

But often there is no gesture gentle or clever enough
to burn her to life before she's ready. And so the soft surrender

as I avoid disappointment, as I slip quietly from bed
to dress, to leave her half of the freshly made coffee
ready in the pot, and take my place among the day,

kneeling in the garden under the low light of morning,
waiting for the warmth of her hand upon my back.

What We Set in Motion

I.

Months out from my bout, I return home
after training deltoids and biceps to push

past the letdown of exertion—to never
stop throwing punches. Our baby boy

bides time in L's belly, two weeks late,
and she smiles, names me her *gentle boxer*

as I shadow my way down the hall
toward the shower. The next day,

after zero centimeters worth of progress,
she sends me back to the gym to spar,

to save my mind from running
the unnecessary laps. I spend round after

round risking and taking damage,
in search of that perfect left hook

to the body, that soft midsection crunch.
I land a few home and feel the accuracy

moving deeper than mechanics,
burying itself in the blue memory

below. Inside the ring I sweat out everything
but bob and weave, but balance and breath, bearing

each combination's bad intent, until brutality
blossoms into something almost beautiful.

II.

And then it's time—as in the dark, we're in it:
maternity wing of the hospital, the lengthening
hours of our son's slow arrival. As in the dark,
a contraction's wave ends, the wash of pain receding,
and L leans back into the rocking chair, back
into the chasm of exhaustion, eyelids
locking her exit from the room. I squat before her
and wait, her body buoyed in the open sea of labor,
as in the dark. My gaze fixes on the map
of monitors, scanning that pixilated horizon
for the next contraction's approach. When it does,
as in the dark, her eyes flare inside the room
once more, hands raising to clasp
behind my neck, as in the dark. I hear the moan
of her spirit bearing this being into light, and I lift
her loaded weight, place pressure
on her hips and say, *give me everything,*
darling, as in the dark. There is no word for the infinite
divide between my desire and my inability to rock
this boy's burden from her, to rock her from the tides
of hurt he's riding in on—this is all her. As from the dark,
as from the sea, another wave builds inside her,
and I send whispers across water, coaching her deeper
into the swallow of its force, calling it *what we want,*
calling it *love* or *joy* or *peace,* as in the dark, barely trusting
each moment that moves her further from this shore,
where I wait for her, to plant our son into these arms.

III.

When they tell us no more fluids. When they tell us time
has scorched the well of his arrival. When urgency cuts through

each gowned voice in the delivery room, the ghost in L's face
says *let them*, and so we let them mine him by fire—with and through fire.

Restraints. No breath. Regional anesthesia. No breath. Nerve block.
Incision. Hemorrhage. And then he adds the sharp thunder of his cry

to the elements. They place him at the altar of her chest. With one hand
free to touch the curl and moisture of his hair, smoke clears from her smile.

IV.

In the nursery, this new kind of quiet
stretches itself inside the plastic, hospital-issued bassinet,

and I stare at my feet—
a sudden fear over the distance down

to them, over having no prayer for looking
into our son's face, years from now, finding

it thinner, the flesh pulled tighter
around the cathedral of his skull,

the mind behind his eyes more
like ours, more tacked to the brittleness

of yesterday, days stacking into months,
memories like seeds spilled across another year.

What's the ritual for forgiving ourselves
the mortal promise we set in motion,

pressed between the floral sheets,
planting his life's fabric into death's seam?

The Epistemology of Preposition

—after A. Van Jordan

Of 1. "during": As in the 28th day of July, of 2011, L finishes lifting the 30th and final hour of our son's getting here—and now I can talk in few tones other than the sweetest day of my life. 2. "being or coming from": As in L has come to me by way of Florida, of Cuban heritage, of parents who left one country's darkness for another's. She smiles in the gray rain of my Seattle, holds my hand. 3. "belonging to": More than the sound of skin, more than the clave of tongues, more than the music, L misses the smell of *churrasco, arroz con pollo, moros y maduros, pasteles y cortaditos* spinning in the blue Miami air. When our son nurses, I imagine him tasting the fleshy pulp of head-sized mangoes, banana hearts bursting in the backyards of barrios, oranges rolled in coffee-brown hands. 4. "concerning; about": I know of grief. My father taught me of want, of waiting—that you can die of waiting. 5. "having or containing": Of course, I'll take a piece of L's bread, a glass of her wine, of her water, the tender country of her abdomen.

Upriver, Downstream

—for J

I read the water, and the edges
of the water, august poplars

casting shadows along the bank. Insect
hatches sometimes bloom

straight from the riffles—all of it
a wayward map to the trout

flexing just beneath the long arch
of my fly-line querying the current.

Alone, I rifle streamers through pockets
deep enough to hold fish large

as memory. With others, I will wade
waist-deep all day, for the small

paradise of watching someone
run their fingers along the belly

of what was once impossible
to touch. And release everything back.

—⁘—

Notes

Epigraph 1: From Li-Young Lee's poem "Goodnight" (*The City in Which I Love You*, 1990).

Epigraph 2: From Stanley Plumly's poem "Grievers" (*Now That My Father Lies Down Beside Me: New and Selected Poems, 1970–2000*, 2001).

"What I Mean When I Say *My Name Is Nobody*": This title borrows from the 1973 film *My Name Is Nobody*, directed by Tonino Valerii and Sergio Leone (uncredited).

"Unfledged": Epigraph from Robert Hayden's poem "Those Winter Sundays" (*Collected Poems of Robert Hayden*, 1966).

"Teaching Twelve-Year-Olds the Trail of Tears": Italicized sections taken from the film series *Trail of Tears: A Native American Documentary Collection* (Dir. varied, 2010).

"What I Mean When I Say *Diaspora*": Epigraph from Robert Hass's poem "Meditation at Lagunitas" (*Praise*, 1979).

"The Epistemology of Preposition": This poem owes a special debt to A. Van Jordan's poem "from" (*M-A-C-N-O-L-I-A: Poems*, 2005).

Some of this book's experimental punctuation was influenced, in part, by my reading of Lyrae Van Clief-Stefanon's *] Open Interval [* (2009).

—⁓—

Acknowledgments

I gratefully acknowledge the editors of the following publications where these poems first appeared, sometimes in earlier forms:

basalt: "King County Metro";

Burnside Review: "The Epistemology of Birds" and "From the Unsent Letters: To Klamath Falls Correctional Facility";

Cave Canem Anthology XIV: Poems 2012–2013: "Call Me Now";

Chicago Quarterly Review: "Instructions for a Fourth-Grade Report on Texas" (as "A Third Grader Draws Texas") and "What I Mean When I Say *Chinook Salmon*";

The Collagist: "What My Father Might Say, If I Let Him Speak";

Conclave: "Write the Memory of Throwing the Stone" and "I Dream of Meeting Myself, Age Seven, County Fair Field Trip";

Crazyhorse: "Revising the Storm, 1991";

Dogwood: "What We Set in Motion";

The Greensboro Review: "The Epistemology of Marriage";

Hayden's Ferry Review: "Meditation at a Pennsylvania Diner: Early Morning" and "Like This, For a Reason";

The Los Angeles Review: "The Epistemology of Gentleness";

The Massachusetts Review: "My Last Love Poem for a Crackhead, #23," "What I Mean When I Say *Farmhouse*," and "Divorce Means";

Mid-American Review: "The Discipline of Waking Love";

Mississippi Review: "The Epistemology of Rosemary";

New Madrid: "What I Mean When I Say *Truck Driver*," "What I Mean When I Say *Diaspora*," and "Unfledged";

New South: "Farmer's Market Sweet Plums: Apology to the Flower Lady";

Nimrod International Journal: "The Epistemology of Preposition" and "Upriver, Downstream";

[PANK]: "Venison" and "What I Mean When I Say *Forever*";

Prism: "More than Forgery";

The Rumpus: "If the Moon Were My Lover" and "The Newakum River";

RiverLit: "The Epistemology of Hospitals";

Sycamore Review: "What I Mean When I Say *Elijah-Man*";

THRUSH: "Write the Memory of the Girl Dancing in Apple Blossoms";

Wisconsin Review: "A Poem for God" and "Dear Destruction";

ZONE 3: "What I Mean When I Say *Roller Pigeon*".

"How Can I Be 1/32nd Blackfeet?" was selected by Jerry Brunoe to appear in *Toe Good Poetry*'s rolling Indian Summer Series, dedicated to Native voices and perspectives.

"Unfledged" and "What We Set in Motion" were republished in *The Feminist Wire*.

"What I Mean When I Say Farmhouse" was chosen by Ellen Doré Watson, Deborah Gorlin, and Lee Edwards as the winner of *The Massachusetts Review*'s 2014 Anne Halley Poetry Prize.

"What We Set in Motion" was chosen by Adrian Matejka as the winner of *Dogwood*'s 2013 First Prize in Poetry.

"King County Metro" was chosen by Nicole Cooley as the winner of the 2012 Leonard Steinberg Memorial/Academy of American Poet's Prize.

"What I Mean When I Say *Elijah-Man*" was chosen by Nikky Finney as the winner of *Sycamore Review*'s 2012 Wabash Prize for Poetry.

My overwhelming gratitude to Peter Conners, Jenna Fisher, Melissa Hall, and the staff at BOA Editions for their commitment to poetry/poets and for their savvy editorial direction.

And to Dorianne Laux, for noticing . . .

My deepest regards for the many teachers/fellow writers responsible for leavening craft, clarity, and conviction throughout this manuscript, *especially* Robin Becker, to whom I owe a great debt, as her warm faith and committed foresight nudged me in all the right directions; for Julia Spicher Kasdorf and her wisdom and kindness; for Todd Davis and Charlotte Holmes; for David Biespiel and Roger Weaver; for Jerry Brunoe and the other original Toe Goods: Kevin Hockett, Eric Noack, and Malynda Shook; for the nurturing arms that the Cave Canem Foundation have opened to poets and, in particular, for the 2012 cohort of CC Fellows and Faculty; for F. Douglas Brown; for William T. Langford IV; for Penn State University's MFA program and graduate students, especially Kim Andrews, Sarah Blake, Rachel Mennies, and Daniel Story; for Sarah RudeWalker; for Moura McGovern. I'd also like to thank Penn State's Institute for the Arts and Humanities and the Center for American Literary Studies for their support of my work.

And there are others that I am surely forgetting—them too . . .

My love to family/friends for their encouragement, *especially* to my mother, Ramona, who taught me the difficult grace of measure in many things, and to my brothers, Edwin and Cary, and my sister, Nikki—the beloved core to my motley tribe; to Adam Haley, Jeffrey Gonzalez, and Lynne Feeley—their brilliant models of caring continue to make me a better person; to John Secreto; to James McClure—both my angling and my health have benefited from our countless hours spent together on the water; also, still somehow, to RL and to my father, wherever/whatever they may be in the world.

And forever, Lissette, whom I cherish beyond words . . .

Lastly, while I don't yet know how or whether to apologize to those who have been called to testify under the liberal subpoena of creativity, I hope they realize this book's affection, if awkward, for all its figures.

—〰—

About the Author

Geffrey Davis grew up in Washington and holds degrees from Oregon State University and The Pennsylvania State University. His work has appeared in *Crazyhorse*, *Hayden's Ferry Review*, *The Massachusetts Review*, *Nimrod*, *Sycamore Review*, and elsewhere. Davis has received the 2013 Wabash Prize for Poetry, the 2013 Dogwood Prize in Poetry, the 2012 Leonard Steinberg Memorial/Academy of American Poets Prize, and fellowships from the Cave Canem Foundation and Penn State's Institute for the Arts and Humanities. *Revising the Storm*, winner of the 2013 A. Poulin, Jr. Poetry Prize, is his first book of poetry.

—⁓—

BOA Editions, Ltd.
The A. Poulin, Jr. New Poets of America Series

No. 1 *Cedarhome*
Poems by Barton Sutter
Foreword by W.D. Snodgrass

No. 2 *Beast Is a Wolf with Brown Fire*
Poems by Barry Wallenstein
Foreword by M.L. Rosenthal

No. 3 *Along the Dark Shore*
Poems by Edward Byrne
Foreword by John Ashbery

No. 4 *Anchor Dragging*
Poems by Anthony Piccione
Foreword by Archibald MacLeish

No. 5 *Eggs in the Lake*
Poems by Daniela Gioseffi
Foreword by John Logan

No. 6 *Moving the House*
Poems by Ingrid Wendt
Foreword by William Stafford

No. 7 *Whomp and Moonshiver*
Poems by Thomas Whitbread
Foreword by Richard Wilbur

No. 8 *Where We Live*
Poems by Peter Makuck
Foreword by Louis Simpson

No. 9 *Rose*
Poems by Li-Young Lee
Foreword by Gerald Stern

No. 10 *Genesis*
Poems by Emanuel di Pasquale
Foreword by X.J. Kennedy

No. 11 *Borders*
Poems by Mary Crow
Foreword by David Ignatow

No. 12 *Awake*
Poems by Dorianne Laux
Foreword by Philip Levine

No. 13 *Hurricane Walk*
Poems by Diann Blakely Shoaf
Foreword by William Matthews

No. 14 *The Philosopher's Club*
Poems by Kim Addonizio
Foreword by Gerald Stern

No. 15 *Bell 8*
Poems by Rick Lyon
Foreword by C. K. Williams

No. 16 *Bruise Theory*
Poems by Natalie Kenvin
Foreword by Carolyn Forché

No. 17 *Shattering Air*
Poems by David Biespiel
Foreword by Stanley Plumly

No. 18 *The Hour Between Dog and Wolf*
Poems by Laure-Anne Bosselaar
Foreword by Charles Simic

No. 19 *News of Home*
Poems by Debra Kang Dean
Foreword by Colette Inez

No. 20 *Meteorology*
Poems by Alpay Ulku
Foreword by Yusef Komunyakaa

No. 21 *The Daughters of Discordia*
Poems by Suzanne Owens
Foreword by Denise Duhamel

No. 22 *Rare Earths*
Poems by Deena Linett
Foreword by Molly Peacock

No. 23 *An Unkindness of Ravens*
Poems by Meg Kearney
Foreword by Donald Hall

No. 24 *Hunting Down the Monk*
Poems by Adrie Kusserow
Foreword by Karen Swenson

No. 25 *Big Back Yard*
Poems by Michael Teig
Foreword by Stephen Dobyns

No. 26 *Elegy with a Glass of Whiskey*
Poems by Crystal Bacon
Foreword by Stephen Dunn

Colophon

BOA Editions, Ltd., a not-for-profit publisher of poetry and other literary works, fosters readership and appreciation of contemporary literature. By identifying, cultivating, and publishing both new and established poets and selecting authors of unique literary talent, BOA brings high-quality literature to the public. Support for this effort comes from the sale of its publications, grant funding, and private donations.

The publication of this book is made possible, in part,
by the special support of the following individuals:

Anonymous x 3
Nin Andrews
Armbruster Family Foundation
Angela Bonazinga & Catherine Lewis
Bernadette Catalana, *in memory of Irving Pheterson*
Anne C. Coon & Craig J. Zicari
Jenna & Stephen Fisher
Anne Germanacos
Suzanne Gouvernet
Michael Hall
Sandi Henschel, *in honor of her daughter Rachel Astarte Piccione*
X. J. & Dorothy M. Kennedy
Keetje Kuipers, *in memory of Maximillian Veracity Kane*
Jack & Gail Langerak
Boo Poulin
Boo Poulin, *in honor of Sandi Henschel*
Deborah Ronnen & Sherman Levey
Steven O. Russell & Phyllis Rifkin-Russell
Jillian Weise